Raising Lazarus
The future of organised labour

by

David Coats

FABIAN SOCIETY

Contents

The Fabian Society

The Fabian Society is Britain's leading left of centre think tank and political society, committed to creating the political ideas and policy debates which can shape the future of progressive politics.

With over 300 Fabian MPs, MEPs, Peers, MSPs and AMs, the Society plays an unparalleled role in linking the ability to influence policy debates at the highest level with vigorous grassroots debate among our growing membership of over 7000 people, 70 local branches meeting regularly throughout Britain and a vibrant Young Fabian section organising its own activities. Fabian publications, events and ideas therefore reach and influence a wider audience than those of any comparable think tank. The Society is unique among think tanks in being a thriving, democratically-constituted membership organisation, affiliated to the Labour Party but organisationally and editorially independent.

For over 120 years Fabians have been central to every important renewal and revision of left of centre thinking. The Fabian commitment to open and participatory debate is as important today as ever before as we explore the ideas, politics and policies which will define the next generation of progressive politics in Britain, Europe and around the world. Find out more at **www.fabians.org.uk**

About the author

David Coats is a member of Hackney South and Shoreditch CLP and associate director of an employment research and consultancy organisation. From 1999-2004 he was Head of Economic and Social Affairs at the TUC.

Fabian Society
11 Dartmouth Street
London SW1H 9BN
www.fabians.org.uk

  Fabian ideas
Series editor: Jonathan Heawood

First published 2005

ISBN 0 7163 0618 2
ISSN 1746-1146

British Library Cataloguing in Publication data.
A catalogue record for this book is available from the British Library.

Printed and bound by Bell & Bain, Glasgow

Introduction

Come with me, then. Let's go backwards. Backwards in time. Back to a country that neither of us would recognise, probably. Britain 1973. ... A world without mobiles or videos or playstations or even faxes. A world that had never heard of Princess Diana or Tony Blair, never thought for a moment of going to war in Kosovo or Iraq. There were only three television channels in those days. ... And the unions were so powerful that, if they wanted to, they could close one of them down for a whole night. Sometimes people even had to do without electricity. Imagine!

Jonathan Coe, *The Rotters Club* (2001)

This is not an obituary for the trade union movement. It is a challenge to trade unionists to face today's realities and take the radical decisions needed to reverse their decline.

The conventional wisdom is that unions are finished. Membership, at 6.4 million, is half what it was 25 years ago. Unions represent 29 per cent of the workforce, and their strength in the public sector (58.8 per cent) masks their weakness (17.2 per cent) in the private sector. For the first time, workers who have never been members outnumber current and former members put together. Politically, the relationship between union leaders and the Labour Government seems rooted in mutual incomprehension. The Government extols dynamism and flexibility; the unions demand security and protection. Each side believes it knows the tune that the other is secretly humming—'do we really have to deal with these dinosaurs'? against 'it's our party and we'll whine if we want to'. The set-piece annual disagreements at party conference now often serve only to highlight the unions' weakness and lack of influence.

Some believe that the unions are so close to death that, like Lazarus, their revival depends on a miracle. This is a problem for the centre-left, not only because of the relationship between Labour and the unions, but because union decline reshapes the balance of power between employers and employees. It enhances employers' freedoms and leaves many employees with no opportunity to shape their own working lives. Social democrats have always argued that industrial democracy and social democracy go hand in hand. This is because we see work as a fully human activity that engages all our skills, talents, capabilities and emotions, and because we emphasise voice and autonomy as sources of self-respect. To deny workers their voice is to deny them control over their lives. If workers are silenced, the employment relationship will become a purely economic transaction.

Yet unions are in retreat across the developed world. If centre-left parties are to be electorally successful, they must build coalitions well beyond their traditional source of support in the organised working class. Inevitably this has become a source of considerable tension. Whilst organised labour may continue to be a progressive force in society, centre-left parties everywhere are struggling with the dilemma of maintaining the support of the unions and appealing to a more aspirational electorate.

It is easy to reach the rather depressing conclusion that nothing can be done: 'trade unions are doomed and the left had better get used to it'. My purpose in this pamphlet is to show that there are good reasons for optimism. Membership decline is not inevitable, and unions remain the masters of their fate. After all, a basic tenet of social democracy is that we reject the crude economic determinism of Marxists and market fundamentalists. At the core of our being lies the belief that we have more opportunities to shape our destinies than the arid theories of either left or right allow. Unions would be unwise to wait for a messianic deliverance or to adopt the Micawberish view that 'something will turn up'. What is needed is a dispassionate assessment of the situation, a willingness to jettison outmoded ideological or cultural baggage, and the disciplined implementation of an agenda that appeals to the massed ranks of the unorganised.

So what possible reason can we have for believing that trade unions enjoy anything other than bleak prospects? The most compelling answer is that workers still display strong support for the idea of collective action. They have an almost instinctive understanding that the employment relationship is characterised by an inequality of power between employers and employees, and they know that co-operation is essential if they are to influence critical employer decisions.

The failure to translate this latent collectivism into resurgence of membership may say more about the unions than it does about British society's enthusiasm for collective action. If the unions are to capitalise on their latent support they must consider whether there is something fundamentally wrong with their brand, product and marketing strategy. In particular, they should note that the rhetoric of struggle, strikes and strife has little purchase on the opinions of employees who care more about 'getting on' than 'getting even'. Potential members are also put off by a sense that unions are stuck in the past, fighting battles in a class war that is of little relevance to most people today.

The TUC's own research shows that workers want unions to be both independent and co-operative, rather than militant and confrontational. Unfortunately, some recently elected general secretaries seem determined to head in the opposite direction. They have suggested that a crude adversarialism—the 'fighting back' strategy—is the route to renewal. This displays little understanding of the dynamics of labour market change and the radical implications for organised labour.

In the age of McDonald's and the Apple Mac, we have more 'McJobs' at the low-skills end of the service industries, and more 'MacJobs' in the

3

new knowledge economy. The labour market has polarised over the last 25 years and now has the shape of an hour glass, with more jobs at the top and bottom, and a shrinking middle. This explains why unions internationally are in decline, regardless of whether public policy is pro- or anti-union. The 'middling' jobs that are rapidly disappearing from the landscape used to be the backbone of trade unionism, and membership decline results from a failure to adapt to these changes. Unions have so far found it difficult to move either upmarket to recruit the more highly skilled, or downmarket to represent the low paid and exploited.

This argument will surprise many British unionists who argue that only labour law reform will lead to membership growth. 'Release us from the shackles of Thatcherism and you will see a surge in union membership' they say. This emphasis on the role of the law is a rather surprising admission of weakness, suggesting the unions' deep-rooted scepticism that they can be the agents of their own revival. Nevertheless, the international evidence is very clear: public policy is not the critical factor in union decline or resurgence—although it can accelerate the trends. If unions are failing to grow in benign economic conditions then they have nobody to blame but themselves. Attributing continued stagnation to Conservative anti-union laws is a neat but unconvincing argument that deflects attention from the need for a serious effort to answer two central questions: 'what are we here for?' and 'how can we grow?'

The unions' ability to meet these challenges has wider political implications. If decline continues unabated then it will eventually call into question the constitutional link between the unions and the Labour Party. Raising this issue always touches raw nerves. There is nothing in British politics quite so neuralgic as the Labour/union link.

Let me make it very clear that I believe in maintaining a strong relationship between organised labour and the Labour Party. Nevertheless, membership decline and union restructuring raise a series of legitimate questions about the precise nature of the link. In particular, the proposed merger between Amicus, the TGWU and possibly the GMB could lead to two men controlling more than 40 per cent of the vote at party conference. It should be clear that the future health of the relationship between government, party and unions depends on the answers the unions give to fundamental questions about their role, strength and legitimacy in the economy and society. If unions are growing then there will be much less pressure for a period of constitutional scrutiny.

Nevertheless, we can see the instability in the union-Labour relationship that could lead to a bitter divorce. Formerly moderate unions now find themselves beached on the wilder shores of anti-government leftism whilst formerly left unions now find themselves, sometimes, as voices of reason. An ex-Communist who had never held national office until his election as general secretary leads Amicus, one of the UK's largest unions. The general secretary of PCS (the largest civil service union) is a self-confessed Trotskyist—although permanent revolution appears not to be one of his central collective bargaining objectives.

The stakes are high and the costs of failure prohibitive for both sides. An objective assessment of the Warwick concordat between the major unions and the government looks, in retrospect, less like the dawn of a more positive and authentic partnership, and more like a pre-election attempt to paper over the cracks. With campaign pressures over, it is back to business as usual, with limited co-operation and intense conflict. The Warwick commitments themselves are relatively narrow—focused on changes to employment law that will be moderately helpful to the unions but will do little to transform British workplaces. The unions are beginning to make demands well beyond the limits of Warwick— including the return of lawful secondary action.

If unions and government remain ships that pass in the night, both sides will be incapable of diagnosing what is wrong in Britain's world of work. Without sustained dialogue there can be neither a shared analysis nor an agreed prescription. The terms of debate are not difficult to define: we know that many people are working longer and harder; stress is reaching epidemic proportions; employment insecurity is widespread and there is strong evidence that the quality of working life has declined over the last decade. These are problems for both unions and government—yet in their mutual distrust they are missing the opportunity to build a progressive consensus in the workplace, to address questions of low pay and equal pay, income inequality, working time and flexibility, training and skills, anti-discrimination and the role of worker voice institutions.

Effective co-operation is infinitely preferable to petty squabbling, a joint effort to tackle the big policy challenges infinitely superior to procedural wrangles at Labour Party conference. In short, government and the unions must devise an accurate ideological compass or both risk finding themselves lost at sea.

This argument is rooted in the belief that Britain needs an effective and responsible trade union movement, representing workers across the economy and working closely with government and employers to solve shared problems. The Labour Party can certainly benefit from a strong link—whether constitutional or otherwise—to trade unions that are representative of the workforce and valued by employers, whose legitimacy is not in question. This requires union renewal. Just as the Labour Party had to go through a painful exercise of political reinvention in response to social and economic change, so unions must embark on a similar journey or run the risk of continued marginalisation and eventual irrelevance. Unions need their 'Clause IV moment' too.

The purpose of this pamphlet is therefore unashamedly political. It seeks not just to analyse the problem but to work out an agenda to address it. The objective is not merely to criticise union strategies but to work out how to make them more effective. The argument attempts not just to inform the debate but also to contribute to a new mobilisation within the trade union movement and Labour Party of those who believe that we can forge a shared progressive vision for the world of work. There is no inevitability in politics—or economics. The answer will depend on what we within the labour movement can do to bring about the necessary changes.

The need for a new generation of trade union modernisers has never been greater. If we do not heed the call today, we will quite probably find that it is too late tomorrow. Unions have one final opportunity for revival, and government one last chance to establish a fairer and more inclusive labour market. It would be foolish, and a tragedy for the left, to throw this away. It is not just that a lifetime working for and thinking about trade unions has left me deeply committed to their cause. It is that the broader prospects of Labour in power in seeking to create and embed social change will be much diminished if the weakness of the trade unions and the thinness of government-union relations are not reversed. The Labour Party and the trade unions must now take the challenges they face and the causes of the tensions between them out of the 'too difficult to think about' box. We urgently need more clarity about the questions that both party and unions need to answer together, or we run the risk that our political opponents will one day soon answer them rather differently.

"

1 | The state of the unions

The future for private sector unionisation is bleak indeed. Perdition is
more likely than resurgence

David Metcalf (2005)[1]

Unless they are truly representative of the modern British workforce, today's unions risk becoming worse than irrelevant. If
membership continues to fall at current rates, and media-
hungry leaders continue to strike confrontational poses, then unions
will become a counter-productive force in labour relations, working
against their members' long-term interests and diminishing their credibility with both employers and the wider public. This will place the
Labour-union link under intolerable strain, as both sides struggle to
justify the special relationship between a party which seeks to represent
British society as a whole and an unrepresentative and anachronistic
network of decaying organisations.

Does it have to be this way? Are the unions doomed to continued
decline or can they achieve a resurgence of membership and a renewed
self-confidence? These are important questions, not just because the
answers will determine the quality of working life for millions of
employees, but also because sustaining the relationship between
unions and the party depends on a revival of union membership and
organisation.

The findings of the 2004 Workplace Employment Relations Survey paint a challenging picture in this context:

> Employees [in 2004] were less likely to be union members than they were in 1998; workplaces were less likely to recognise unions for bargaining over pay and conditions; and collective bargaining was less prevalent. ... [U]nion involvement in pay setting and the joint regulation of the workplace [was] very much the exception in the private sector and in smaller workplaces.[2]

Remember that the period 1998-2004 was characterised by positive changes in individual employment law, the adoption of the social chapter of the Maastricht Treaty and the implementation of the new legislation on trade union recognition. Nonetheless, union membership continued its inexorable decline. In 1979 the TUC had more than 12 million members, today the figure is 6.4 million. Union density (the percentage of the workforce in membership) stood at 49 per cent and collective agreements determined the pay and conditions of around three quarters of employees. The comparable figures now are 28.8 per cent and 35 per cent, and these are largely sustained by significantly better union organisation in the public sector (58.8 per cent density; 71.6 per cent coverage) than the private sector (17.2 per cent density; 20.5 per cent coverage).[3] Even these disturbing figures probably conceal the true extent of decline in the private sector, where union organisation remains strong in the de-nationalised industries (energy, water, steel, rail etc) and weak almost everywhere else. A like-for-like comparison between the private sector in 1979 and 2004 would force an observer to conclude that much of the private sector is utterly union free.

The unions, moreover, are ageing organisations. Density among 16-24 year olds is only 9.7 per cent, whereas density in the 35-49 and 50+ groups is 34.7 per cent. Other research has shown a declining propensity among young workers to join trade unions. A worker who started their career in a non-union environment is now extremely unlikely to become a trade union member at any point in their working lives.

Union membership in the private sector has been on a gentle downward path over the last eight years, falling from 19.2 per cent to 17.2 per cent. In the public sector, density has fallen too, from 60.9 per cent to 58.8 per cent, although the number of members has increased from 3.4 to 3.7 million, reflecting the growth in public sector employment since the election of the Labour government.

The concentration of membership in the public sector is a further source of weakness. The situation could get more difficult as the growth of public spending slows and pressure on the public finances intensifies. Continued battles between government and public service unions augur badly for the future, and public sector unionism could be under real threat if the Conservatives return to power with an anti-union prospectus. Spending the next four years in a series of running battles with a Labour government will expose public sector trade unionism to the stronger likelihood of a Conservative assault.

The higher density of union membership among women (29.1 per cent) than men (28.5 per cent), reflects a catastrophic decline in male union membership rather than an upsurge in support among women. It is explained too by the concentration of union membership in the public sector where density among women is higher than for the private sector.

The TUC's own research from 2001 shows that 'never members'—those who have never had any connection with the trade union movement at any point in their working lives—are now the largest group of workers in the UK economy (see Figure 1).

An equally challenging finding emerged from the TUC's projection for the development of union membership from 1999 to 2017. This explored three scenarios for structural change in the economy and identified an irresistible downward trend in membership (see Figure 2). The current level of density (28.8 per cent) is consistent with the most pessimistic level for 2005 that was predicted by the model in 1999, suggesting that overall union density may fall as low as 20 per cent by 2017.

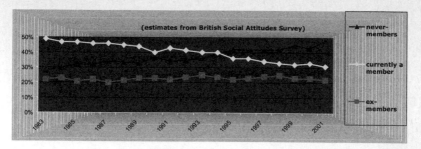

Figure 1: The Growth of the 'Never Members'
(percentage of employees)

Figure 1: Key Findings
- Never members are now the largest group of workers in the UK economy
- Trade unions are becoming increasingly distant from most people at work
- Media images will shape the never members' perception of what unions do—will these workers have a favourable opinion of trade unions as a result?

Of course, all this assumes that unions continue with their present strategies and remain unsuccessful in building their membership in growing sectors of the economy. The last eight years have been characterised by economic conditions that in the past would have fuelled union growth, but we have witnessed decline in the private sector and stagnation in the public sector. The omens for renewal are not good.

It is important to understand that this is not just a British phenomenon. Unions appear to be in decline across much of the developed world. The principal exceptions are those countries where unions play a role in the administration of the unemployment benefit system (Belgium, Denmark, Sweden), or where a social pact has entrenched the union role in national life (Ireland, for example, although even here the unions are struggling to maintain density as the economy expands). The corporatist structures of the post-war period remain in place across most of the 15 countries in the pre-expansion EU, but falling union

11

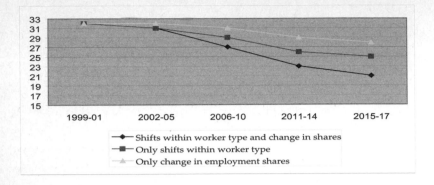

Figure 2: Scenarios for Union Density 1999-2017, percentage of employees (estimates by Bryson from British Social Attitudes Survey)

Figure 2: Key Findings

- These projections suggest continued union decline for the foreseeable future
- The current level of membership is consistent with the most pessimistic projection of membership decline
- Decline is not inevitable if unions can develop a strategy that appeals to 'never members'

membership could threaten the robustness of these arrangements. The raw phenomenon of union decline appears ubiquitous although public policy has influenced the speed of the decline.

A declining appetite for collective action?

This body of evidence indicates the scale of the challenge that unions face. The harsh truth is that trade unions today seem irrelevant to most employees and employers in the private sector. Workers who have entered the labour market since 1980 are increasingly unlikely to be trade union members, and workplaces established since 1980 are less likely to recognise unions for collective bargaining.[4]

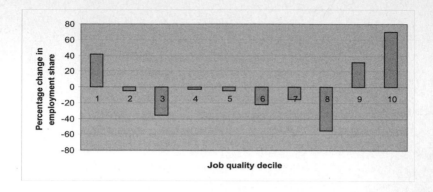

Figure 3: The 'Hour Glass' Labour Market—Job Change by Income
Decile 1979-99 (Source: Dickens et al, *The Labour Market
Under New Labour* [2003])

Figure 3: Key Findings

- Job growth over the last twenty years has been at the top and bottom of the labour market: we have more McJobs and more MacJobs in the UK and an 'hourglass' shaped labour market
- Trade union strength used to be located in those 'middling' jobs that are rapidly disappearing from the landscape
- Unions need to respond to the trajectory of labour market change by recruiting workers at both ends of the hourglass. This demands a sophisticated approach with different union 'offers' for different groups of workers

The decline of manufacturing, the gradual disappearance of the manual working class and the erosion of a distinctively working class intellectual tradition have conspired to create a much less favourable climate for organised labour.[5] Moreover, the shape of the labour market has changed dramatically over the last 25 years. Put simply, the labour market now looks like an hour glass, with more 'good' jobs at the upper end of the earnings distribution, more low paid 'bad' jobs at the bottom and a shrinking middle (**Figure 3**).[6] Nevertheless, we can say with confidence that on average job quality in the UK has increased over the last three decades—more people have 'good jobs' today than in the 1970s.[7]

This trend is driven principally by technological change and can be found across the developed world. Routine but relatively well-paid jobs that would have been done by people are now being done by machines. Wage inequality has grown everywhere as a result of the 'hour glass' phenomenon—even in a country like Sweden with a relatively narrow dispersion of earnings.[8]

Many of the 'middling' jobs that are slowly disappearing from the landscape are in precisely those industries and occupations where unions have historically been strong. Put another way, we are witnessing the disappearance of what the Victorians would have called the 'respectable working class', a social formation that historically provided the backbone of the trade union movement and is now being replaced by a burgeoning middle class and a growing group of people with low paid, low skill, low quality jobs.

This hollowing out is reinforced by what some researchers have described as a 'declining appetite' for trade unionism among workers. While much of the membership decline of the 1980s was the result of structural change in the economy and the difficulty of securing recognition for collective bargaining, decline in the 1990s is better explained by the fall in union density in organised workplaces.[9] People are not leaving unions in their droves but are simply failing to join in the first place, even in workplaces where unions are recognised. The hollowing out of the workforce and the declining appetite for trade unionism are in fact two sides of the same coin: new jobs are being created in those occupations where unions have historically been weak, whilst unions' organisational structures limit their ability to follow employment growth, particularly in more highly skilled occupations, with effective recruitment campaigns.

It would be wrong, however, to say that membership decline is explained by a declining public commitment to collective action. The TUC's research reveals that people have an instinctive understanding

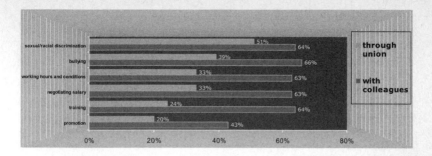

Figure 4: How do non-members in unorganised workplaces want issues to be dealt with? (percentage of non-union sample BWRPS 2001)

Figure 4: Key Findings
* Workers understand that the employment relationship is inherently unequal
* They know that they need to work with their colleagues to have any influence over employer decisions
* This 'latent collectivism' is not yet manifested in a desire for union membership. 'Never members' often find it hard to see the relevance of unions to their situation

that the contract of employment is inherently unequal and that, in the words of the new Clause IV, 'by the strength of our common endeavour we achieve more than we achieve alone'. There is robust evidence that confirms a high degree of latent collectivism among unorganised workers.

Half of the non-union workers in the British Workplace Representation and Participation Survey were asked whether they would like to deal with a range of workplace problems on their own or with colleagues and the other half were asked whether they would like to deal with the same problems on their own or through a union. The results show a strong collectivist orientation but a much weaker union orientation (see Figure 4). In other words, people appreciate the logic of collective action and believe that they can only make progress if they

15

collaborate with their colleagues but fail to see that trade unions have any relevance to the process.

This should not surprise us, because most of these people are 'never members'. Almost all that they know about trade unions has been gathered through the media. This leaves never members open to persuasion of the benefits of union membership, but it poses a challenge too, forcing unions to make their 'offer' more relevant and appealing.

Further evidence of this latent collectivism can be found in the responses to another of the BWRPS questions which asked whether people wanted to be represented by a union, a union and a works council, a works council only or had no desire whatsoever for representation (**see Figure 5**). This suggests that around a third of non-members are likely to resist any appeal from the trade unions but only 5 per cent of non-members want union representation alone. This is a very challenging finding that should encourage serious reflection across the trade union movement.

Why do so few non-members express enthusiasm for trade unions when 62 per cent evince some support for collective voice? Is the problem simply that these workers are ignorant of what unions do? Or are they genuinely sceptical that union representation alone would be effective in changing employer behaviour? This suggestion is reinforced by the very strong support among union members for representation through a union and a works council. In other words, it appears that union weakness is driving both union members and non-members to look elsewhere for a guarantee that consultation will be a meaningful process. Furthermore, a significant group of non-members—women, in particular—are left cold by the unions' public image. Not merely 'male, pale and stale', today's unions may appear 'aggressive, rooted in declining industries and male, pale and stale' and therefore 'nothing to do with me or my experience of work'.

The TUC's 2003 report, *A Perfect Union?*, documented the sources of union effectiveness in the workplace and revealed that union members give equal priority to unions protecting workers against unfair treat-

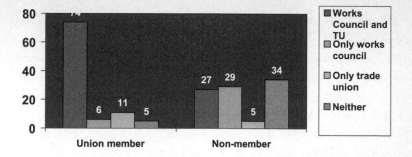

Figure 5: All in all do you think your workplace would be better with...?
(percentage of employees BWRPS 2001)

Figure 5: Key Findings

- There is a strong commitment to some form of collective voice among two-thirds of non-members

- Only 5% of non-members want union representation alone rather than some other kind of 'voice'

- Union members are strongly in favour of statutory rights to information and consultation (a works council) to address the weakness of collective bargaining and union representation

ment and working with the employer to improve productivity and performance (**Figure 6**).

There is an emphasis on procedural fairness and a belief that unions play a valuable role as a 'strong friend in the workplace' when people get into difficulty. To that extent the 'insurance' element of the standard union offer continues to appeal to workers. But there is also a very clear understanding that only successful workplaces can offer good conditions of employment and unions have a responsibility to work with employers to improve organisational performance.

What is most striking about the findings, however, is the low priority given to making work interesting and enjoyable. This is a genuine surprise, given that unions have always aspired to influence the quality of work in the broadest sense. At first glance it appears that workers

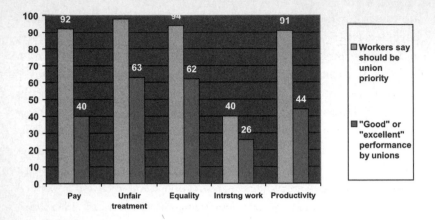

Figure 6: Assessment of union effectiveness
(percentage of employees in unionised workplaces, BWRPS 2001)

Figure 6: Key Findings

• Workers endorse the standard union priorities of pay, equality and protection against unfair treatment

• Unions working with the employer to improve productivity and workplace performance has the same priority as securing fair pay increases and bonuses

• Workers know that they will not have high quality jobs unless their workplace is successful and the union works with the employer to achieve this goal

have lost faith in the ability of unions to make the experience of work better. In large measure this reflects a lack of union power and a narrowing of the bargaining agenda.

Once again, however, there is some cause for optimism. Those unions which are highly rated for working well with the employer to improve productivity also have high ratings for making work interesting and enjoyable. It seems clear that those unions who collaborate with the employer on work organisation, job design and joint problem solving

18

are valued by their members. In other words, the most effective unions have developed a robust, co-operative relationship with the employer, and exercise genuine influence over critical decisions. Far from being a betrayal of working class interests, a relationship with the employer characterised by trust, respect and mutuality is what most members want from their unions. There is little endorsement here for the adversarial simplicities peddled by some recently elected general secretaries.

This evidence lends strong support to those who argue that unions should be more about 'getting on' than 'getting even'. Any strategy based on treating all employers as mean and exploitative will not entice the many 'never members' who feel broadly positive about their experience of work, who like and respect their employer, identify with the mission and purpose of the organisation but also believe that things could be better.

We must also remember that more women will join and remain in the labour market over the next decade. This ought to shape union agendas in the general direction of 'mutual gains', if only because many of the issues relating to gender equality do not lend themselves to a simple zero-sum model of collective bargaining. Achieving equal pay is as much about the patient work of reforming pay structures as it is about challenging the employer to be less sexist—as the Agenda for Change agreement in the NHS has proved. Ending gender segmentation in employment demands cultural change and skills development as well as the agreement of equalities policies. Promoting more flexible working patterns and ensuring that these are not a fast track to career death is another process that seems more amenable to collaboration with employers than overt and sustained confrontation. Similarly, responses to the recommendations of Margaret Prosser's Women and Work Commission (due to report in February 2006) cannot simply be a matter of legislation on the one hand and an intensification of union 'equalities rhetoric' on the other. It is very unlikely that the Commission's report will endorse 'fighting back' as a model for the achievement of workplace equality. Unions need to remember that many women are 'never members' with a low tolerance threshold for macho posturing. They are unlikely to be enthused or inspired by middle-aged male union leaders engaging in aggressive exchanges with either employers or government.

Rather similar points might be made about race equality at work, where the achievement of genuine equal opportunity demands an effective partnership between unions and employers.

So where does this leave the unions? We can be reasonably certain that the structural change experienced by all mature capitalist economies over the last 25 years has weakened the foundations of union power across much of the developed world. The extent of the change has been greater in the UK than in many other countries, which is obviously a testament to the effectiveness of Thatcherism. But the truth remains that no unions have yet found an adequate response. Those which claim to have done so, like Andy Stern's Service Employees International Union in the USA, are operating in a labour market where a very traditional union offer—'join us and we will help you get even with the employer'—has real resonance with poor, exploited, black or Hispanic manual workers in low pay, low skill jobs. It is wrong to believe that there are lessons here for organising a more highly qualified, better skilled workforce, although some British unions—most notably the TGWU—seem to be falling into this trap. As Ron Todd once perceptively commented, affluent workers today are unlikely to be enthused by the slogan 'brothers and sisters let me take you out of your misery!' This salutary lesson ought to be the cornerstone of union strategy in the future.

Nevertheless, we should keep in mind the phenomenon of the hourglass labour market: there are more good jobs and more bad jobs, but more good jobs than bad jobs. Unions are not going to succeed in becoming more representative of today's workforce if they only focus their attention on the rough end of the labour market. Most people do not work in rotten jobs, and the number of jobs at the 'quality' end of the market is rising. On the other hand, low paid workers want representation too, and trade unions have an obligation to protect those most at risk. Unions must therefore tailor their strategies to the pattern of labour market change.

In other words, unions must go upmarket to recruit the better paid and better qualified and at the same time move downmarket to recruit those doing low paid, low quality jobs in private services. This is by no means as straightforward as it sounds. The strategy needs to be nuanced and sophisticated with a range of offers to appeal to different groups of workers. The fiery rhetoric of class solidarity may energise those employed in 'bad jobs', which partially explains the SEIU's success in the USA and the supposed success of Bob Crow's RMT, but it may also have the effect of reinforcing negative stereotypes, which could make unions less attractive. Indeed, an aggressive adversarial stance is not even necessarily the best strategy to recruit the low paid and disadvantaged. The shop workers' union USDAW has adopted a very different approach to the recruitment of low paid part time workers, emphasising lifelong learning, career development and widening opportunity. This has proved successful and the union is growing. Even if one believes, against all the evidence, that 'fighting back' is the only strategy for the rough end of the labour market, it is unlikely to work with airline pilots, senior civil servants, telecommunications professionals or any of that expanding group that we might collectively describe as 'knowledge workers'.

66

2 | The new unionism: rising to the organisational challenge?

For too long trade unions have listened too much to the gaffer and have been too close to government. Preaching all the rosy talk of social partnership. 'New Labour will sort it out.' Now I believe the tide has turned. There is a new mood of determination in the movement. We are no longer wasting our time looking for generous employers—I've never met a generous employer in my life. No longer waiting for ministers to deliver justice. We are working to rebuild our organisation, our membership, our unity and our fighting spirit.

Tony Woodley
General Secretary, TGWU
Durham Miners' Gala, 2004

For most of the 1990s the TUC's strategy was clear: unions should invest more in organising the unorganised and build resilient high trust relationships with employers. 'Organising' and 'partnership' were presented by the TUC leadership as two sides of the same coin—one was worthless without the other. It was argued that unions depended for their success on strong workplace organisation and employer support for the union role.

This short-lived attempt at a win-win strategy was not without its tensions. The left saw 'partnership' as irredeemably right-wing and collaborationist, associated with 'sweetheart' deals and an attempt to cosy up to ultra-Blairite modernisers. For the right, 'organising' was either a pointless romanticisation of the importance of self-sustaining workplace activism or a Trojan horse for small and unrepresentative vanguard sects to spread their message across the movement.

These questions of organisational strategy eventually became subsumed in a wider argument about the relationship between unions and government. A sense of disappointment with Labour created a rising tide of dissatisfaction with 'partnership' to the extent that few trade unionists will now use the term and expect to be taken seriously.

Nevertheless, partnership had and still has much to commend it. The intention was clear: partnership could maximise the influence of unions with government and management, and minimise the possibility of catastrophic disagreement. It was an attempt to create the space for sensible compromises to be reached, and part of a determined effort to move the UK closer to the 'European social model'. Not so much about 'listening too much to the gaffer', as Tony Woodley suggests, but more a case of 'getting the gaffer to listen'.

By failing to give the advocates of partnership consistent support, the government unwittingly undermined the modernising forces in the trade union movement. It was very easy for the left to argue that 'partnership' was a blind alley. There could be little doubt that many employers remained hostile to unions and that the government had caved in to employer pressure by diluting the recognition procedure, the minimum wage and the new employment rights for individuals. Modernisers found themselves squeezed between a 'triangulating' government, unsympathetic employers and a resurgent left.

In the Manichean struggle for the soul of British trade unionism, the left are currently in the ascendant. A crude version of the 'organising model' has replaced 'partnership', and 'fighting back' has replaced co-operation. Yet despite their recent successes, the left are bereft of new ideas to promote union growth. Deploying the rhetoric of class struggle may enthuse the dwindling band of union activists who can still remember the 1970s, but it does little to stimulate interest among younger, more highly qualified workers or workers in private services. Left unions have adopted an essentially defensive posture, consoling themselves that they can continue to behave as if the world has not changed.

The left also argue that they have an intuitive understanding of 'what workers want', which is superior to any of the evidence produced using the robust methodologies of social science. The finding that workers want both protection and partnership is interpreted as nothing more than right-wing propaganda and therefore unworthy of serious attention, as is the suggestion that strong workplace organisation goes hand in hand with co-operation and employer support for the union role. Some general secretaries place a high value on 'research' that confirms their prejudices, but feel free to disregard any findings that might require them to think. Indeed, they sometimes have a disturbing tendency to see prejudice as fact.

Organising for what?

It requires real determination to disregard both the triumph of New Labour and Thatcherism's radical break with the past. As a weary insider has commented, treating today's workforce as if everybody is a militant, male car worker living in a council house on Merseyside ignores the social changes of the last 30 years. What then should unions do to face these transformed social realities?

Union organising is both a marketing exercise and an exercise in mobilisation: unions want workers to join, buy their product and continue to pay subscriptions. Unions need to be clear about what they are trying to sell and who they are expecting to buy. Unions must be able to answer the 'what are we here for?' question with conviction, clarity and persuasiveness, and have a clear understanding of their potential market or markets. They need to have an explanation of why membership should be attractive that is based on evidence rather than prejudice, myth or 'gut feeling'.

Unions are broadly suspicious of the language of brands, marketing, focus groups and the like—just as the Labour Party was until the advent of Peter Mandelson. Yet their failure to grow—in relatively benign conditions, with a high level of support for collectivism—must suggest that there is something fundamentally wrong with the union brand, product and marketing strategy. The ritualised exchanges between rival enthusiasts for 'organising' and 'partnership' are themselves an exercise in displacement activity that excuses both parties from having to address these major questions in an open and honest spirit.

Assuming that unions can respond with a degree of confidence, they must determine what it is that keeps workers in membership. Inevitably this poses further questions about the nature of collective bargaining and relationships with employers. In the past, it was clear that a fairly significant wage premium was associated with union membership—so it was perfectly valid to say: 'join a union and your pay will rise'. This is no longer the case, partly because of the decline of collective bargaining, but also because of the intensification of competition in product markets.[10] It is unlikely that we will see the return of a large union wage premium in the near future. This being so, what is the principal advantage of union membership?[11]

The simple answer is that unions continue to have a powerful 'sword of justice' effect. Unionised employers are more likely to comply with employment regulations, have narrower pay differentials (so less wage inequality), a narrower gender pay gap, a better record on equalities policies and fewer workplace accidents. There is also evidence to show that unionised workplaces have a better record on vocational training. These are not insignificant advantages and speak directly to the priorities of union members, as discussed earlier.

What about relationships with employers? We have already seen that union members favour a relationship with the employer that allows for collaboration to improve productivity and performance. Equally, we know that employees whose employer supports the union role are far more likely to see their unions as effective.

25

It is common sense that the process of producing goods and services demands a high degree of cooperation between workers and employers. Without this, no customers would be served and no orders would be filled. Workers do not go to work looking to pick a fight with their employer; most people just want to get on with their jobs. This is not to suggest of course that conflict can never occur—of course it can. Indeed, conflict is nothing more than a consequence of the inequalities of power inherent in the employment relationship. Workers want independent representation, which is precisely what unions offer and, when necessary, a collective countervailing force to the power of the employer.

But life at work is not and cannot be a constant battle. Unions must accept that they have to appeal to employers as well as employees and that, in the absence of a high degree of employer support, unions will always struggle to maintain membership and legitimacy.

This is demonstrated by studies examining the impact of unions on the industrial relations 'climate', which show that the worst of all possible worlds involves a weak union that raises members' expectations but lacks the wherewithal to influence employer decisions.[12] For both employers and employees, strong unions are better than weak unions.

Evidence from the Workplace Employee Relations Survey shows that most non-union employers are either neutral about or indifferent to trade union organisation, although unions report that opinions tend to harden when an organising campaign begins.[13] Employer opinion is malleable, however. If unions can demonstrate that they play a constructive role in those organisations where they already have collective bargaining rights, then non-union employers are much less likely to be hostile. The difficulty of course is that, just as with the 'never members', many employers have no experience of trade unions at all and will be principally influenced by their public image. A trade union campaign for 'a voice in every workplace' is easily interpreted by some employers as 'a Bob Crow in every workplace'—an outcome that even the most enlightened will be keen to resist.

Things can only get better?

Returning to our theme of brand, marketing and product, part of the union 'offer' is to help workers avoid the vicissitudes of today's more challenging labour market. This is an opportunity for unions to provide support, encouragement and a forward-looking agenda. Yet the messages emerging from this year's TUC Congress would put any 'never member' into a state of extreme anxiety: 'manufacturing is collapsing'; 'jobs are being lost daily'; 'the government is not doing anything like enough'; 'pensions are in crisis'; 'public services need more investment'; 'the government has a secret plan to privatise public services'. All this is the common currency of any union conference. Some unions have inverted the doctrine of Voltaire's Dr Pangloss: for them, all is for the worst in this worst of all possible worlds.

This is both surprising and predictable. Surprising because the UK economy has performed well in the last eight years, unemployment is low, employment growth has been robust, GDP growth relatively strong and inflationary pressures weak. In comparison to the situation that unions confronted through the recessions of the 1980s and 1990s this seems to be a very benign environment. What might unions say when the economy really does hit some choppy water?

What is surprising too is that some unions seem to have only the sketchiest understanding of the darkening economic horizon. With the exception of the problems confronting British manufacturing, there was nothing on the TUC's agenda that reflected concerns about sluggish growth, the problems of the eurozone economy, the apparent deterioration in the public finances or the likely consequences for public spending.

The inevitable result is that the government gets little or no credit for its achievements. This confirms the widespread sense (promoted by conservative newspapers and some broadcast journalists) that New Labour is failing in its mission to improve public services. Equally worrying is the implicit confirmation that all unions can do is complain about decisions over which they have no influence.

On the other hand, this tone is predictable in that the default mantra for many unions now is to 'accentuate the negative, eliminate the positive'. Unions were so bruised by the experience of Thatcherism that their whole culture has become defensive, insular and depressive. But once again, this can only create the impression that 'we fight and we lose'. Unions could make considerable progress simply by celebrating their achievements. They could point out for example that the world has changed for the better since 1997 and that unions can take much of the credit. Without their campaigning there would be no minimum wage, no union recognition, no strengthening of employment rights, no social chapter, no new rights for working parents, no investment in union based workplace learning and no union modernisation fund. Unions should also take credit for their specific collective bargaining achievements, including the elimination of the 'two-tier workforce' in public sector contracting, the workforce remodelling agreement in schools and Agenda for Change in the NHS. Associating the union brand with success is essential for a resurgence of both membership and influence.

Beyond the rhetoric: a positive union strategy

None of these questions are new. Indeed, they provoked a lively debate on the left 27 years ago when Eric Hobsbawm published *The Forward March of Labour Halted*. At the heart of Hobsbawm's argument was the notion that 'the forward march of labour and the labour movement appears to have come to a halt in this century about twenty-five or thirty years ago.'[14]

Hobsbawm dated the decline of the labour movement to the period 1948-53. He identified a range of factors that had contributed to the 'halt', including the decline of the manual working class; the end of 'a common style of proletarian life'; the transformation of British capitalism so that 'the factors that determine the workers' conditions are no longer, to any major extent, those of capitalist competition';[15] the growth in the number of women at work; immigration and the rise of racism among the working class; increasing sectional differences between workers, which led to a decline in class consciousness and solidarity; and declining electoral support for the Labour Party.

One might see this as a belated recognition by the Euro-Communist wing of the Communist Party that the questions posed by Labour's revisionists in the 1950s—most notably Anthony Crosland—were the right ones to ask.[16] How could the labour movement adapt to a society characterised by widespread abundance, the growth of consumerism, the decline of deference and the desire for greater personal freedom? It was only in the 1990s that Labour began to be comfortable with trends that had first been detected 40 years earlier. Indeed, the early phase of New Labour represented a determined and wide ranging effort to answer the revisionist question. Far from being a centre-right project there were many on the left who understood the need for change, of whom Robin Cook was an outstanding example. Much of the progress made under the leadership of Neil Kinnock was also focused on adapting the party to contemporary British society.

Trade unions were often uncomfortable with this process, failing to back Tony Blair as leader and opposing the amendment of Clause IV. They remain uncertain whether they need to go through a similar exercise to achieve their own revival. To this extent many trade unions are genuinely 'Old Labour', finding it difficult to accept that the world has changed, and preferring the comfort of conference rhetoric to a radical reappraisal of their role.

With the exception of the progress made on gender equality, most trade unions today look much as they did 40 years ago. A visit to any union conference will confirm this impression: the fashions may have changed but the people, procedures and agendas are fundamentally the same. To outsiders, the proceedings of the TUC and union conferences are as mystifying as the court rituals of Byzantium or imperial China.

The language and myths of the movement are redolent of a period before the arrival of general affluence. A sentimental attachment to the past is a significant obstacle in the path of union renewal. 'Old Labour' in this sense is dead and ought to be given a decent and respectful burial. Of course, this does not mean that unions should forget their roots and their history, but it does mean that future strategy should be determined by a sober assessment of the evidence rather than by reference to precedent, sacred texts or myths, however uplifting they may be. There is a strong case for saying that union revival is impossible without a symbolic 'Clause IV moment'.

Whether the large general unions can respond to this argument remains an open question. Some might even reject the premise that there is a problem, while others would see this as a philosophical discussion of little relevance to union renewal. Even so, it is possible to detect the beginnings of a new approach. Some unions are showing a genuine willingness to adapt to confront the more difficult challenges that people face in the world of work.

How might we characterise these challenges? There is very clear evidence that people believe that they are working harder today than they did a decade ago. There is an increase in dissatisfaction at work across all occupational groups, particularly with workload, working time and the intensity of work.[17] Somewhat surprisingly, employment insecurity also seems to have increased, despite strong employment growth and stable job tenures.[18]

Put simply, British workplaces have become less humane in the last decade. There appears to be a degree of discontent about pay and we also know that there is a high level of unhappiness with the degree of influence that people have at work.[19] Combined with the accelerating pace of change, this is creating a sense of employment insecurity that would otherwise be inexplicable. Why should people feel uncertain about their futures when job tenures have been stable for a prolonged period and unemployment is low? It can only be that workers feel powerless in the face of what seem to be ungovernable forces of nature.

We also know of course that average job quality is rising, so the situation is not unremittingly awful, despite some union rhetoric to the contrary. We might conclude our assessment by saying that a high level of job satisfaction coexists with genuine concern about what is happening in the world of work. People have complex views about their situation and are unlikely to respond to simplistic appeals.

This demands some subtle presentation of the trade union case which emphasises the traditional 'insurance' function of a trade union; the role of unions in dealing with dissatisfaction about pay; the ability of unions to improve access to learning and development; a determined focus on making work less 'stressful' by humanising the workplace; and the commitment of trade unions to giving workers effective voice over critical employer decisions.

To express the same argument slightly differently, what unions need to do is to inspire the unorganised with confidence that the world of work can and should be better, that an accelerating pace of change may be unavoidable as markets integrate and competition intensifies but that workers can still influence the process. Unions need to establish themselves as institutions that can help people navigate the shoals of a more challenging world of work.

Growing unions are doing this already and have displayed a real capacity for innovation. These unions have established themselves as custodians of professional or craft standards, offer job search and career counselling services and advice on employment contracts.

Providing fairly extensive labour market services to members is not a recent innovation. Indeed, services of this kind were most well developed in sectors with closed shops, where unions effectively controlled the supply of labour. But even though these precise arrangements are unlikely to return, there is no reason why unions should not try to revive their role as labour market intermediaries. Community is making a determined effort to reconceptualise what a trade union should be. It has a strong track record of delivering access to training, particularly for those made redundant as employment has fallen in the steel and clothing industries, and its next step is to develop an employment and welfare rights advice service, so that members see the union as a resource that enables them to manage critical events in their lives.

Connect, the union for telecoms professionals, offers advice on individual contracts, job search and career counselling services. Prospect, a union with its roots in the civil service which now represents technical and professional staff in both public and private sectors, has moved in the same direction. The Chartered Society of Physiotherapy is both a trade union and a professional association; it publishes the learned journal of the profession and provides members with information about job opportunities.

'Getting on not getting even' and the humanisation of work can be detected in some recent and groundbreaking collective agreements. This is the inspiration behind the Workforce Remodelling agreement in schools, which has released teachers from routine tasks and created a ladder of opportunity for support staff. The same is true of the Agenda for Change agreement in the NHS, which has the explicit objective of eliminating gender pay inequality and should create scope for enhanced career progression for lower paid staff.

Unions have also made huge strides in widening access to learning and development—often with explicit government support—which gives members a profound sense that their union can provide access to skills development to sustain employability. Unison's Return to Learn programme has created real opportunities for workers with low levels of formal qualifications to return to education. CATU, the ceramics union, has a highly successful basic skills programme and it is genuinely moving to hear members say 'my union has helped me learn to read and write'.

USDAW, the shop workers' union, has developed an innovative agreement with Tesco that has had the effect of significantly widening the bargaining agenda. Matters on the table for discussion include creating a genuine culture of lifelong learning, with wider opportunities for career progression, breaking the 'glass ceiling' that excludes women from managerial posts and making a serious effort to tackle violence in the workplace. In this case the employer's view is quite explicit. The union is the 'conscience of the business' and an agency that helps the employer to sustain the company's strong performance. Union membership has grown significantly since the agreement was concluded. This is a fine example of a union organising lower paid and lower skilled workers using the language of aspiration—enabling members to develop their careers and acquire new skills is at the heart of USDAW's strategy. Similarly, tackling violence in the workplace is essential in ensuring that workers are treated with respect. This agreement is of great significance, principally because the union has proved that relatively low paid workers respond with more enthusiasm to an offer that is about improving the workplace than to an offer focused solely on 'fighting back'.

It is also the case of course that the possession of appropriate skills enables workers to cope with pressure, reduces the experience of stress and leads to higher quality work, better health and longer life expectancy.[20] All these examples show that unions can make a big impact on individuals' life chances—in some cases by offering opportunities for transformational change. They also demonstrate that some unions understand the nature of the polarising labour market, recognise the need for a common agenda based on fairness and opportunity and also understand the need to appeal to different groups of workers using different strategies. In other words, these unions have successfully moved both upmarket and downmarket, tracking the trajectory of labour market change.

Such achievements are uncelebrated, rarely receiving any media coverage, but they demonstrate that unions across the TUC are pursuing more than the simplistic adversarial agenda of tabloid myth. While these unions may not have big battalions they do have energy, imagination and commitment. These are qualities that should be highly prized by a movement that is otherwise in decline. Sometimes size may matter, but it is also the case that smaller organisations can be more adaptable, swifter to respond to events and closer to the concerns of their members.

Union Structure: 'Circling the Wagons' and the impact on the TUC

This view is likely to prove unpopular with the large general unions. Amicus, the TGWU and possibly the GMB are all now focused on the so-called mega-merger scheduled for 2007. No doubt they see merger as an effective strategic response to membership decline and in principle the rationale is persuasive: merger will lead to economies of scale, more efficient deployment of limited resources, less inter-union competition, better services to members and a solid foundation for growth.

In contrast, recent research suggests that most of the advantages claimed for large-scale union mergers have not materialised—principally because vested interests in each of the merging organisations have obstructed the path.[21] Far from providing a foundation for growth, mergers have created huge, unwieldy organisations, lacking a sense of identity (members don't know what they belong to) and characterised by perpetual negotiation between different interest groups. Indeed, Paul Willman has suggested that large-scale mergers have compounded the problems and are unlikely to generate significant membership growth in the future:

> The essentially consolidatory and impoverished conglomerate may be less a mobilization tool than a defensive and risk averse accommodation poorly equipped to mount an assault on the growing non-union sector.[22]

In particular, large-scale mergers have generally led to a weakening of union balance sheets, with the merged organisation being poorer and less well resourced than its predecessors. This raises some rather profound questions about trade union structure and reinforces the view that unions are often victims of their own history. British trade union structure has always been messy, illogical and apparently unworkable— although unions have muddled through in practice. The problem with the merger process of course is that it does little to overcome these weaknesses. Many mergers have had a political rather than an industrial logic and they reproduce the messiness of union structure within one organisation. There is a persuasive case for mergers that create focused industrial trade unions, with a strong foundation in a particular sector and the ability to operate at both ends of the hourglass. But the current proposals fall well short of this ideal and to create a more logical structure would require the demerger and reconstitution of many of the TUC's affiliates. The new merged union will be trying to do far too much with far too little. The expectations are high and look likely to be disappointed.

Far from being a route to resurgence, the proposed Amicus, TGWU and GMB merger could therefore reinforce the phenomenon of membership decline. It constitutes a 'circling of the wagons', an essentially defensive strategy, which may lead to internal squabbling at a time when attention should be directed outwards to the wider world.

It is worth remarking that union growth in the past has never been generated by huge conglomerate organisations. Instead, it has been new organisations or previously small unions that have proved successful in organising workers in growing parts of the economy—see for example the growth of white-collar trade unionism in the 1960s, the early efforts to organise unskilled workers in the 1880s and 90s or the growth of general unions in early part of the twentieth century, when Ernest Bevin brought together a large number of small, medium-sized and growing organisations to create the mighty TGWU.

Whatever the impact on union membership, there can be little doubt that the mega-merger, if successful, will have a huge impact on the TUC. On current figures the Big Four (Amicus, Unison, TGWU and GMB) have 3.9 million of the 6.4 million members, and the new merged union would have 2.6 million members alone.

If the TUC is to maintain its current broad membership in the future then the two large unions will need to display rather more sensitivity to the views of their smaller and specialist counterparts. It may be unpopular to raise the issue in public, but there is a real concern, expressed sotto voce today, that if two unions have the whip hand over all decisions then smaller unions will be unable to make their voices heard.[23] A continued turn to the left could also be problematic. Those organisations which continue to be 'moderate' may be unhappy if association with a more militant, aggressive stance damages their relationships with employers.

If the merged union proves unable to accept the principles of pluralism and diversity that have been the hallmark of British trade unionism in the past, then some professional/specialist unions may seek a looser confederation where they are able to act together more effectively to articulate their distinctive views. The risks are significant, as the recent split in the US trade union movement has proved, but a failure to forge a sense of shared purpose based on a clear understanding of how trade unions can best operate across the whole of the labour market is fatal to trade union unity. In other words, the new merged union and perhaps Unison too should recognise that they have something to learn from their smaller and more specialist counterparts.[24] Most importantly, it is essential that the new union understands the importance of differentiated union strategies that allow organised labour to operate at both ends of the hourglass. To suggest that those unions suspicious of 'fighting back' are lacking authenticity and commitment or are guilty of 'collaborating' with employers is hardly likely to foster a spirit of solidarity.

66

3 | Political strategy: implementing the Warwick agreement

Our slogan could be: "What do we want? We don't know. When do we want it? Now!"

Billy Hayes
General Secretary
Communication Workers' Union[25]

The union movement is quick to seize on its opponents' weaknesses and slow to address its own. It is aided in this by the media, which—when it notices the unions at all—focuses almost exclusively on stories about a split with Labour, not on the real challenges facing organised labour. This adds to the impression—shared by nostalgic unionists—that unions still have it within their power to make or break governments. The reality falls some way short of this dubious aspiration. Jack Jones and Hugh Scanlon may have been major national figures in their day but their modern counterparts are barely recognised by the general public. Were it not that some unions have a constitutional role in the Labour Party, union stories would be well below the media horizon. Events that would have received widespread national coverage even a decade ago are now confined to the margins of the broadsheets. There is an overwhelming sense that unions just do not matter much any more.

Indeed, the combined effects of social change and membership decline have made organised labour a much less important element in British social democracy. Unions were once the predominant constituency in the Old Labour coalition, with 90 per cent of the votes at party conference. Now they find themselves a shrinking and sometimes marginal element in the New Labour coalition. Unions ought to reflect upon their straitened circumstances and consider how best they can exercise political influence. Perhaps most importantly they need to be clear about how they can use a prolonged period of Labour government to establish a progressive consensus in the workplace that can withstand an electoral defeat, which, if not imminent, is certain to happen at some point in the future.

Affiliated and non-affiliated unions

It is important here to distinguish between the position of those unions affiliated to the party and those which are not. Only those unions affiliated to the party were signatories to the document agreed at the Warwick policy forum. Affiliated unions are obviously more politically engaged than non-affiliates and they may often use the TUC as a vehicle for pursuing arguments that will also be carried forward through the party's own structures. This can create a degree of confusion between the position of the TUC and the position of party-affiliated unions. Disagreements about Warwick implementation are essentially matters of dispute between the party and its affiliates. Other unions are largely bystanders with no direct voice in the process. A focus on 'delivering Warwick in full' may frustrate non-affiliated unions who believe that their priorities are equally worthy of consideration.

It is undeniable, however, that both affiliated and non-affiliated unions need to have a clear political strategy for the delivery of some practical objectives. Affiliated unions will be looking for a durable constitutional settlement which enables them to work through the party's structures on both manifesto implementation and policy development. Both affiliated and non-affiliated unions have an interest in establishing a consensus about the union role in the world of work that can withstand a change of government. In part this may be about changes in the law, but it is far more important that public policy values unions as institutions and promotes collective bargaining and the worker voice aspects of the union role. Unions need to be confident that their position in the labour market will not be called into question following a Conservative victory. If they secure this objective then we really can say that Labour and the unions have created a progressive consensus in the workplace.

Political strategy—to Warwick and beyond

By the time of the 1997 election there was a measure of agreement between Labour, affiliated unions and the TUC about the policy agenda for the world of work. Trade union recognition, the National Minimum Wage, stronger individual employment rights and signing the social chapter of the Maastricht treaty were all matters of consensus that found their way into the manifesto. While the implementation of these commitments caused considerable tension between the TUC and the Government there can be little doubt that the first term produced significant victories for Britain's unions. Unfortunately the same cannot be said of the second term, where there was no such clear agenda and arguments raged relentlessly about the role of the private sector in the delivery of public services.

It was welcome then that both government and affiliated unions recognised the need to identify some common objectives for the third term and that agreement was reached at the Warwick policy forum. On the other hand, even the most optimistic assessment suggests that Warwick was a short term and partial settlement. The unions' strategy was to make the case for a 'shopping list' of policies for inclusion in the manifesto—repeal all the anti-union laws, modify the recognition procedure and so on—in the expectation that they would not secure all their objectives but would at least achieve some of them. To a degree, this reflected the strategy pursued for more than a decade: get some limited and clear commitments accepted through the party's structures and compel the government to deliver. As can be seen from a synopsis of the Warwick commitments (**below**), the unions achieved a great deal. Perhaps more than they expected. On the other hand, some core objectives, such as the repeal of the anti-union laws and the reinstatement of sympathy action, seem as distant as ever and are unlikely to be delivered by this or any other Labour government. We might note too that these commitments are more pro-worker than pro-union and will do little to promote union organisation across the economy.

Nevertheless, the Warwick document does contain some of the most pro-union statements to be found in a Labour policy document for some time. The Government stated its belief that unions are a good thing, because they

> [p]rovide a voice for people at work and contribute to the success of companies and public services. In wider society individual trade unionists make a notable contribution through their service on public bodies, local government and other community bodies.[26]

Warwick makes clear that unions offer voice and therefore procedural justice in the workplace, work constructively with employers to improve organisational performance and can be a valuable source of social capital. Furthermore:

> Labour believes in strong, modern unions that are representative of the diverse workforce, and which play a role in securing the success of workplaces. Labour wants to work in partnership with the trade union movement to help such unions grow.[27]

Given the weakness of unions in the private sector, and their inability to cause wage inflation or block necessary change, it may seem surprising that the Government is still keen to engage with them. There are some more obvious reasons why the Government should want to maintain relations with unions in the public sector, where unionism remains relatively strong, but the Government's commitments are to unions generally rather than those where they happen to be the employer.

One can only conclude therefore that this Labour Government is seeking to develop the union role for ideological reasons—either because unions are 'a good thing' in the workplace, correcting imbalances of power and building social capital, or because national policy is likely to be more effective (and effectively legitimised) if it is agreed by the social partners—witness the success of the National Minimum Wage and the critical role played by the Low Pay Commission. In other words, these judgments are informed by principles and values, which, if properly articulated, could provide a solid foundation for a new relationship between government and unions.

A cynic might find this analysis far too positive, and claim that the government is keeping the unions on life support, with regular blood transfusions through the Union Learning and Union Modernisation Funds, and lacks the will to switch off the machine.

Alternatively, it could be said that the Warwick commitments represent the irreducible minimum necessary to maintain union quiescence during the general election campaign. The apparent enthusiasm for the union role was nothing more than a pre-election rhetorical flourish. New Labour remains committed to an essentially neo-liberal view of flexible labour markets with weak employment rights, feeble unions and a high degree of wage flexibility.

Certainly, there is enough in the Government's rhetoric to justify the latter view, although it is also worth pointing out that this so-called neo-liberal government has presided over the greatest re-regulation of the labour market for a generation. On any conventional analysis the UK labour market has become significantly less flexible since 1997. We have a rising national minimum wage, which sits in the middle of the OECD's index of regulatory toughness, more stringent dismissal rules

Warwick Commitments

New Deal
1   Improve the New Deal, bring in private and voluntary sectors, help specific groups

Jobcentre Plus
2   Innovate and test new approaches to ensure full employment in every region; build on success of JobCentre Plus personal advisers; more focus on the front line

Helping People on Incapacity Benefits
3   Ensure that benefits are set at a level that ensures dignity and security for the sick and disabled
4   Support those on IB who want to work and ensure that careers advice and opportunities are available to older people

Ethnic Minority Employment
5   Implement the Ethnic Minority Task Force report, build on success of New Deal and devolve power to the front line

Making Work Pay
6   Review the impact of the Lower Earnings Limit
7   Keep the Agricultural Wages Board and review its remit
8   Implement the NMW upratings [this is implied rather than explicit, although the government has accepted the Low Pay Commission's proposed upratings for 2005 and 2006] and remind employers that the NMW is a legal minimum and they should aspire to pay well above this rate

New Rights at Work
9   Be alert to any future threat from the BNP and be willing to legislate accordingly—making it easier for TUs to expel racists from membership

10   Extend period for unlawful strike dismissals to 12 weeks

11   Will evaluate project looking at TU organisation and recruitment in SMEs in heating and ventilating sector; will use results as a basis for further discussion [this is in context of the TU recognition procedure and exclusion of workplaces employing less than 20 workers]

12   Support the principle of an EU Agency Workers' Directive and look to reach early agreement with the Commission/other member states on these provisions

13   Implement the deal on the two-tier workforce applying the local government principles to the wider public sector

14   Develop a new compact with contractors and unions on public service employment standards—to ensure that employees 'have access to advice, basic training and skills and trade unions should they wish'

Insolvency and Redundancy

15   Bring forward measures to ensure that during redundancy consultation employers do not take premature action, like the removal of plant, which prejudges the outcome of consultation; review limit on statutory redundancy pay and bring in proposals to raise the limit

16   Examine responsibilities of insolvency administrators towards workforces and their representatives in relation to redundancies or changes in conditions of employment

17   Examine how redundant workers can be given priority access to the New Deal for Skills

Positing of Workers Directive

18   Monitor operation of Positing of Workers directive

Services Directive

19   Support adoption of services directive—although ensure that this does not undermine any of the UK's regulatory frameworks

Safe and healthy workplaces and employees

20   Support HSE's pilots looking at new ways to provide occupational health; undertake an assessment and decide on next steps in developing national policy for occupational health

21   Draft Bill on corporate manslaughter [this happened before the election] and then legislate to ensure that both public and private organisations can be prosecuted for serious criminal offences where they have shown a disregard for the safety of employees

22   Expand the work of local authority Crime and Disorder Reduction Partnerships to tackle violence and anti-social behaviour in and around front-line workplaces

Protecting and improving opportunity for the most vulnerable

23   Look at ways to prevent employers and agencies from holding migrant workers' passports

24   Bring together the social partners to discuss the development of a voluntary comprehensive 'good employment practice standard', perhaps as part of PiP

25   Look for more effective action by enforcement agencies—draw on experience of Telco; examine proposals for an 'Advancement Agency' as developed by John Denham MP and consider the possibility of a dedicated helpline for those with employment problems

26   Bring together social partners in low paid sectors to discuss strategies for raising productivity, health and safety standards, as well as employee pay, skills and pensions

Skills

27   Will consider how industry can properly contribute to the gains they obtain from a higher skilled workforce

28   Build on evidence from JobCentre Plus pilots so that where low skills are a barrier to work job seekers receive the help they need

Work-Life Balance

29   Will develop options to improve legislation on the length and remuneration of maternity, paternity, adoptive and parental leave, examining practice in other European countries

30   Review the right to request flexible working; look at improving the accessibility of parental leave and at options including making this paid time off

31   Will continue to consult with parents and others with the aim of establishing a consensus on the action needed

The long hours culture

32   Take steps to ensure that people can exercise genuine choice about hours of work; consult social partners to identify abuse and 'will introduce any changes in the law that are necessary' (but not remove the opt-out from the 48 hour week); four weeks leave to be additional to 'the equivalent of the bank holidays'

Childcare

33   Extend the 'Extended Schools Childcare' scheme, ensuring that local childcare partnerships work with employers and trade unions to provide the childcare that working parents need

34   Continue to press public and private sectors to carry out equal pay audits and introduce non-discriminatory employment practices; systematic review of factors influencing the gender pay gap, women's opportunities at work, stronger equal pay legislation and the possibility of mandatory equal pay reviews [all now being taken forward by the Women and Work Commission]

Information and Consultation

35   Will offer support to business, especially SMEs, to enable them to implement effectively the new rights to information and consultation

and higher levels of compensation, equal rights for full-time and part-time workers and new rights for working parents.

It would be better to conclude that the UK is developing a distinctive social model, which is neither Anglo-Saxon capitalism, red in tooth and claw, nor the Rhenish model of the social market with its panoply of institutions for co-determination. Unions would be wise therefore to take the Warwick commitments at face value—they are well meant and New Labour really is dedicated to strengthening modern, mature and responsible trade unionism. On the other hand, this does not mean that trade unions have a blank cheque, an open opportunity to demand a new wave of changes to employment law or a free hand to argue for a significant extension of European level regulation. In particular it should be clear that the Government will have no truck with 'fighting back' trade unionism, a return to Scargillite syndicalism or a recrudescence of the lunacies of the 1980s.

Of course there are differences of view in the Government, with varying levels of optimism and pessimism about the prospects for unions to rebuild their membership and influence. Some say that there is no route back for unions in the private sector: the decline in membership has gone too far and the growth areas of employment are in industries that unions have always found virtually impossible to organise; unions will remain strong in the public sector and government will need to take this seriously, but otherwise the party would do well to accommodate itself to the certainty of continued decline. This suggests that while some effort will be made to make the Warwick commitments work, a failure to build effective social partner institutions will not be seen as a catastrophe.

Others have a more positive outlook and believe that those unions growing today can point the way to a wider revival. The new social partner institutions envisaged in Warwick are important because they can build union legitimacy, provided of course that unions behave responsibly and demonstrate a real capacity to make a constructive contribution. Rebuilding the unions is part of the process of rebuilding the party's base. The link with affiliated unions is valuable because it roots the party in the experience of working people and gives Labour a foothold in the workplace.

At present the scales are finely balanced between these two views, with the weight slightly on the side of the sceptics. Neither side could remotely be described as anti-union. They both want unions to thrive in the future. It is simply that one group is more optimistic than the other about the likelihood of union resurgence.

There are already some early signs that cracks are beginning to open in the Warwick façade. Much of this is still concealed from public view and can only be detected from the tone used by general secretaries of the large affiliated unions. A new front has opened up for example, following the Gate Gourmet dispute, as the unions revive the argument about the legality of sympathy action. Further sources of tension include the role of the private sector in public service delivery and whether the Prime Minister should announce his retirement forthwith. All of this is destabilising and will make the rapid implementation of the Warwick commitments more difficult.

An absence of vision

What is most striking perhaps are the limited ambitions expressed by affiliated unions. It is difficult to detect a clear vision of what the world of work should look like after a prolonged period of Labour government, little sense of where unions fit in the picture and no account of how employer support can be secured for a durable settlement in the world of work.

Indeed, union strategy is too often derailed by *causes celebres*—like Gate Gourmet or the earlier Friction Dynamex case where striking workers were dismissed after eight weeks on the picket line—so that events affecting a relatively small number of workers become the over-riding priorities of the movement. This is not to excuse bad practice by employers, but simply to note that hard cases make bad law and that rebuilding the unions' organisational base requires the disciplined pursuit of a clear set of deliverable objectives which address the problems experienced by most people at work.

Perhaps most seriously, the approach of unions affiliated to the party has eschewed any clear articulation of the relationship that they would like to have with government. There is no serious agenda to which both parties are committed beyond the implementation of new forms of labour market regulation, no real commitment to sustained dialogue on the problems that were documented earlier or the challenges facing the country. Yet these challenges are immense and were outlined to a degree by Gordon Brown in his speech to the TUC this year. How can the UK sustain strong economic growth, generate high quality employment and produce goods and services that people abroad would like to buy in a world of intensifying competition and accelerating change?

At this point we might reflect for a moment on the 'Woodley paradox' that seems to be at the heart of some unions' strategies. On one hand we have the view that unions have got too close to government and should stop waiting for New Labour to deliver justice. On the other we have the strongly expressed views that the Government should act to deliver justice by implementing Warwick and reinstating the freedom to take secondary action. One of the justifications advanced by enthusiasts for the mega-merger is that it will give the new union a more powerful voice inside the party—and presumably more influence with government. This does little for unions' reputation for consistency.

The blame for the deteriorating relationship between unions and the government does not lie solely on one side. In the period immediately after the 1997 election, the TUC tried to establish an agenda where effective collaboration with government could lead to the creation of a durable partnership.[28] Priorities included creating and sustaining full employment, plugging the UK's skills gap, improving productivity and building a new model of industrial relations. Much of this was the work of TUC officials who had experience of the Social Contract in the 1970s and who valued the role of the National Economic Development

Council. As I have argued elsewhere, while the Prime Minister may have liked and trusted John Monks, he had little time for other senior union leaders and saw the TUC's offer of a revived corporatism as a risk that was not worth taking.[29] Employers were at best unenthusiastic about social partnership and their opposition combined with New Labour's suspicion meant that the horse fell at the first fence.

Now of course the political environment is more challenging and the Government could benefit from enthusiastic union support in addressing some of the critical policy challenges facing the country. Whether a rather better relationship can be constructed is explored in the next chapter.

Constitutional consequences—what next for the link?

All these considerations inevitably lead to some rather profound questions about the future of the union/Party link. This is dangerous territory, as Stephen Byers discovered to his cost when he tentatively raised the issue with journalists over a fish supper in Blackpool. But the issue has not gone away and will rise to the top of the agenda once again if the Amicus–TGWU–GMB merger becomes a reality.

The Prime Minister has already indicated his willingness to consider the issue and reflected the concerns about a widening gulf between party and unions:

We should consider, with our affiliates, better ways of involving their members in decision-making. A situation where constituency delegates regularly get voted down by a block union vote doesn't do any good for our relationship or credibility. The union relationship is important and we should keep it. In times gone by it has saved the Labour Party from near extinction. But, like everything else, it should be modernised for today's world.[30]

There are two issues for consideration here. The first is a narrow constitutional point: is it right that almost half the votes at party conference should be in the hands of two general secretaries? The second is of deeper significance: what is the purpose of the Labour-union link if trade union membership is on a slow but irresistible downward slope?

There is something inherently undemocratic about the policy of a governing party being determined by two people. It smacks of a return to the smoke filled room, of Tammany Hall, machine politics and a lack of transparency that is offensive to many ordinary voters. Polling evidence suggests that while most trade union members want their unions to have a political voice, there is widespread opposition to the view that trade unions should be able to exercise undue influence over government policy. This has been true since at least the mid 1970s. All unions with political funds have managed to secure continued membership consent through the regular ballots required by law, but few unions have campaigned for their political funds only on the grounds that they have a constitutionally guaranteed seat at the Labour Party's table.

This then brings us to the second question. Can any value be derived from a link with declining institutions that represent principally public sector workers and a shrinking aristocracy of labour in the private sector? The arguments used to justify the link in the past remain strong in principle today. Trade unions can give the party an organic connection to the majority of working people. A constitutional voice for trade unions protects the party against extremism, the political obsessions of the 'chattering classes' and a focus on cultural politics. Unions provide the party with organisational resources during elections—not just money but people too—and create a talent pool from which many MPs and ministers are drawn. The trade union group remains the single largest group inside the Parliamentary Labour Party.

Even those sympathetic to the trade union cause sometimes find it hard to advance these arguments with absolute confidence today. Concerns remain that breaking the link would cut the party adrift from its moorings, that the absence of trade unions from the coalition would drive Labour in the direction of the 'limousine liberalism' that has done such damage to the Democratic Party in the USA and that political weakness would follow. But there is a strong sense that these considerations weigh less heavily in the balance than in the past, not least because if union decline continues the resources available to the party will decline too.

In the past the unions have saved the party from policies that were electorally disastrous. Now they seem to be the architects of policies that the leadership believes to be electorally damaging. This throws into question the historic role the unions often played in restoring the party to sanity after a period of crisis. It is the constituency parties today who are more inclined to support the government and the unions who are more inclined to be oppositionist. Unions run real risks when they find that they are disconnected from majority opinion in the constituencies as happened at this year's conference. Their relative powerlessness is emphasised when resolutions are carried principally with union support and then ignored by government. Equally, it is not constructive for unions to accuse the government of 'betrayal' over Warwick implementation and, at the same time 'betray' Warwick themselves by making demands that are well beyond the scope of the agreement—the return of sympathy action and opposition to the EU services directive for example. If this process is replicated in the future then the unions could find that they have overplayed their hand and the constituency parties will begin to question the constitutional status quo.

All these problems are compounded by some unions' presentation of their relationship with the party as transactional—'we give you money and you give us the policy we want'. Historically this has never been the foundation of the relationship. Unions supported Labour because Labour would run the economy to maintain full employment, invest in public services and improve the social wage. In other words because Labour would govern in the interests of ordinary working people, 'those who work hard and play by the rules', and most working people were either trade union members or covered by collective agreements.

Perhaps we should pose our central question in more straightforward language: can and should the link be sustained in future if union membership is declining and if union and party leaderships are increasingly out of step? My answer is yes, but the process is likely to be messy and fraught with difficulty. Nevertheless, it would be hugely damaging to both party and affiliated unions to engage in a bout of constitutional navel gazing and far better to make a determined effort to put the relationship on a secure footing.

What is required is a process that commits both unions and party to the practical application of shared values and moves beyond the line-by-line negotiation of Policy Forum documents. Drafting the next manifesto demands a very different approach. Most importantly, there must be a genuine exchange of views rather than a ritualistic exchange of positions. Unions should come to the table without a 'shopping list', reach an understanding with government about the problems to be solved and agree the interventions required. It is not simply a matter of the unions dictating and the government responding or the unions making absurd demands and the government resisting. Both sides should learn from the exercise and be confident that what emerges at the end is more than simply 'a deal'. Unions will benefit from a much clearer long-term political strategy and the party leadership a much clearer view about the valuable contribution they believe the unions can make.

Some significant problems could remain even if a more effective process of policy development is agreed. Put crudely, if unions begin to grow then there is little value in reopening the constitutional question, but if unions continue to shrink then the precise nature of the link will need to be reassessed. In those circumstances the party should, at the very least, have a calm and reasoned discussion about where unions fit in the decision making process. The question of voting weights at Conference and in the Electoral College will become unavoidable and a first step may be to align Conference voting weights with the Electoral College weights, giving more power to the constituencies and MPs.

A discussion about the party's constitution may in turn demand an open debate about some state funding of political parties. Indeed, one might say that this is probably a necessary condition for the restoration of faith in our democratic institutions. Both Labour and the Conservatives have been damaged by the unseemly quest for cash and an unfortunate impression has been created that large donations generate policy influence. Allocating some public funds could create a cushion of resources enabling parties to do more than simply maintain the appearance of independence. This does not mean of course that unions could not continue to fund the party, but it would establish that the relationship is not transactional, stemming from shared values and objectives rather than the cash nexus.

The argument made here is clear. The link can continue to be an advantage for both parties if government and unions find a shared sense of purpose and if union membership begins to rise. Unions will be able to maintain their position as an essential, albeit not the predominant, component of the New Labour coalition if they can sustain the argument that they represent Britain at work in all its richness and diversity. The situation will be very different however if the pessimistic predictions of union decline are borne out in reality. In those circumstances the constitutional question will inevitably rise to the top of the Party's agenda.

4 | Is there an alternative? Union futures

Murder, often. Divorce, never.

Jack Jones

No one ever said it should be easy. Unions do not exist to give employers, the government or the Labour Party a soft ride. On the contrary, unions exist to represent their members' long-term interests, to give voice to the voiceless and to help balance the demands of a globalised economy against the needs of workers seeking to support themselves and their families. A strong union movement is essential if we are to maintain this balance, and respond effectively to the neo-liberal assault. It is right too that unions should be affiliated, if they choose, to the Labour Party, whose commitment to workers is evident in the New Deal, the working tax credit and the minimum wage.

But can the unions and Labour really forge a new partnership in the third term? There are three possible scenarios: things get worse and the relationship deteriorates; the status quo continues with an unstable combination of effective collaboration and intense conflict; or party and unions identify some common objectives to create a progressive consensus in the workplace that can withstand a change of government. The third scenario does not mean that government and unions will always agree, particularly given the concentration of union membership in the public sector where government is the employer. But a sophisticated conversation about shared values could lead to the development of a persuasive account of what constitutes a 'good' labour market, with a clear articulation of the role for unions, whether affiliated or non-affiliated. Government and unions would then be able to identify the practical measures needed to bring the vision to reality. Working closely on an agenda where there are clear, shared interests may make it easier to handle profound disagreements when they arise.

Scenario 1: 'Things fall apart, the centre cannot hold'

It is of course possible that the unions will consult their divorce lawyer and decide that they would like to make the marriage work. But as we have seen, disagreements are already emerging around the implementation of the Warwick agreement, and these splits are likely to be compounded by disputes in the public sector about private sector involvement in public service delivery. If the relationship continues to deteriorate along these fault lines, then it is probably destined for irretrievable breakdown.

Scenario 2: Negotiated conflict and limited co-operation

The unions' approach to the government today is characterised by a cocktail of collaboration and opposition. They have engaged successfully with the government on skills strategy through their involvement in the national Skills Alliance and the new Sector Skills Councils. Similarly, unions are deeply embedded in the institutions for managing health and safety at work; they work with the government on public service reform through the Public Services Forum, negotiate the minimum wage level through the Low Pay Commission, have guaranteed representation on the ACAS council and on the equalities commissions and play an increasingly important role in regional development agencies.

Even so, it is difficult to see that unions and government have a common view about the world of work. There is no comprehensive Labour/union story about the characteristics of a 'good' labour market beyond the commitment to full employment, no shared vision of what kind of jobs we need to sustain the UK's prosperity in the future and no shared understanding of the role played by worker voice institutions (whether unions or works councils) in building social capital and promoting social cohesion. The current level of collaboration might be sustained but it is inherently unstable and will always be threatened by the failure to embrace a clear and coherent narrative.

Scenario 3: Towards a progressive consensus in the workplace

The real challenge for both unions and government is to use what will be 13 or more years of Labour in power to build an enduring legacy and transform the culture of British workplaces. Having a clear vision and a set of broad objectives is essential in developing coherent policy. What Labour and the unions urgently need is a well-developed and convincing story about what constitutes 'good work'. Warwick may have seen party and unions through the general election campaign but in itself Warwick is a short-term fix, not a durable settlement.

The government should be interested in this for sound political reasons. No political party has yet developed a clear narrative about 'good work' and the first party to do so persuasively should benefit from a significant electoral dividend.[31]

Government and the unions must develop an accurate ideological compass or run the risk of finding themselves lost at sea. If there is agreement on the course, and clarity about the destination, it will be much easier to articulate the roles and responsibilities of the various stakeholders and deal with attacks from political opponents. Many of the issues that have caused most difficulty over the last eight years could have been managed more effectively if government and unions had agreed on their aims and objectives.

Put simply, the challenge for government and the unions is to develop a 'progressive consensus' in the workplace. This must proceed from the starting point that work is a fully human activity that engages all our skills, talents, capabilities and emotions. Both government and unions ought to be able to agree the conditions that must be met for human beings to flourish fully in the world of work. They ought to be able to work together and build widespread support for a model that delivers both high quality employment and strong organisational performance. The key questions for Labour and the unions to answer are: what constitutes 'good work?'; how can we get more of it in the UK?; and what role do trade unions play in creating sustainable high quality jobs?

This means that both government and unions need to start engaging with what the other is really doing and stop tilting at windmills. It means that government should focus more clearly on the need for a social dimension to match the dynamism of the UK economy—and should make the case for a social dimension at European level too. It means that the unions should stop suggesting that the Government's labour market policies are borrowed wholesale from American Republicans when they quite clearly are not. Unions and government should collaborate closely on the development of a distinctively British social model—and confront those employers who have nothing more to say than 'no more regulation', revealing their unwillingness to accept that there are significant problems in the world of work today.

It means too that government and unions must articulate a shared account of the role of the law and the role of voluntary action. Unions seem to measure their success by the volume of labour law on the statute book. Government on the other hand appears suspicious of 'excessive regulation'. What both need is a comprehensive view of where the balance should be struck between the law and collective bargaining. The problem with reliance on the law of course is that legislation, if it remains controversial, can be easily repealed by an incoming government, although this problem is less acute if the quest for a progressive consensus has been so successful that both employers and opposition parties support a robust employment law settlement.

How might this consensus be built? To begin with, unions and government should jointly address questions of low pay and equal pay, income inequality, working time and flexibility, training and skills, anti-discrimination and the role of worker voice institutions. Both parties must embark on this dialogue with an open mind, and there should be a genuine discussion about how to make progress. Both unions (whether affiliated or non-affiliated) and government are committed to widening opportunities in the world of work. If the slate could be wiped clean and past causes of disagreement forgotten it should in principle be possible to agree a progressive agenda that has real resonance with employees, is supported by a majority of the electorate and is therefore beyond challenge by either employers or opposition parties.

For both unions and government it means abandoning the pattern of unions making an unrealistic demand and the Government responding with a resounding 'no'. Unions need to marshal their arguments and proceed on the basis of evidence, rather than simply asserting that something ought to be government policy because it is already union or TUC policy, and unions have the votes to win at conference. The aim must be to develop a practical agenda where a shared analysis leads to an agreed prescription. That is what deliberative policy making is all about.

What other issues might be the subject of a continuing discussion? Low pay is an obvious example, where the sectoral forums proposed in the Warwick agreement present real opportunities for progress. All that the NMW has done is establish a floor under wages. But what can government, unions and business do together to improve the performance of low pay, low productivity, low skill organisations? If we are really serious about making the UK a dynamic knowledge driven economy then how can we improve the quality of employment at the rough end of the labour market? Developing a discussion of this kind means that unions will feel they have more opportunities to tackle low pay; they will have a more realistic view of the role and limits of the NMW; and will be able to contribute to an agenda that improves the UK's economic performance.

A similar approach might be adopted to the implementation of the recommendations made by the Women and Work Commission. Both unions and government want to eliminate the gender pay gap, enable women to break through the glass ceiling that makes many management jobs men's jobs and end the segmentation of jobs by gender. Given these shared objectives it ought to possible to prepare a programme of action with clear roles for unions and government.

On working time too it is essential that government and the unions adopt a consistent policy for the promotion of family friendly employment and the eradication of excessive working hours. The law will always be inadequate to the task and much will depend on collective bargaining or voluntary action by employers. Once again there is a practical agenda for discussion.

Unions and government also need to reach an understanding about the role of worker voice. This is inevitably a controversial question, not least because of the difficulty of dealing with the CBI. But the issue may have become more manageable for government because the Information and Consultation regulations (I&C) mandate the establishment of consultative committees in non-union workplaces. This makes it difficult for the CBI to argue that the worker voice question is simply about union power.

Progress has been hampered by the Government's reticence about the union role and—contrary to the position of previous Labour governments—its refusal to express a clear preference for collective bargaining as the fairest and most effective instrument for the determination of pay and conditions. It is unlikely that this will change—particularly given the absence of unions from most of the private sector. However, the Government could easily offer more explicit support for a partnership model of industrial relations, and encourage the adoption of such a model in the public sector. The aim must be to send a clear signal that the 'fighting back' approach has little appeal, and that unions need to revive the commitment to workplace partnership that characterised the work of the TUC for more than a decade.

The Government should also advance a rather different argument for I&C. Thus far the case has been made on the purely instrumental grounds that collective and individual voice are good things because they enhance organisational performance. A 'good work' narrative would enable the Government to develop a more profound justification for these measures on human rights grounds—after all, the rights to freedom of association are guaranteed by a plethora of international conventions. Voice is important because it gives workers autonomy, control and a sense of self-respect—all factors that are associated with high levels of employee well-being. Any centre-left party needs to be clear about the conditions under which citizens can flourish in the world of work, and the critical role of worker voice institutions is an essential part of the social democratic story. Once again this is not a new argument: RH Tawney was making the case in the 1920s that any credible model of social democracy demanded a much higher level of industrial democracy.[32]

The corollary of this argument is that unions must accept that they no longer have exclusive rights to represent workers. EU law rests on a foundation of universal rights and offers no privileged status to the union channel for workplace representation.

The universal rights model poses a challenge to those who view I&C as a threat rather than an opportunity, and there is evidence that union scepticism about the potential of the regulations is becoming more widespread. In part this is a consequence of regime change at the top of the big unions. The new general secretaries are much less enthusiastic about I&C than their predecessors and this reduces the scope for the TUC to champion the transformational potential of the new regulations. Nevertheless, the effective use of the I&C regulations must be integral to any union strategy for renewal and growth.

The future of pensions in the UK will rise to the top of the agenda when the Turner Commission reports later this year. Leaving aside the specific recommendations that may be made, it is likely that the Government will need allies to build a consensus around a new settlement. At the moment the unions are wedded to a rather simplistic model of employer compulsion but it is possible that this may change—

they understand the importance of having a Plan B too. This means that there is probably scope for a constructive conversation later in the year about how best to make progress.

Finally, there is the question of productivity and sustainable economic growth. Some progress was made through the TUC/CBI productivity discussions in 2001, but the outcome was rather unsatisfactory and practical implementation of the recommendations has been patchy. Government could take the opportunity to revive the process and enlist unions in tackling the UK's productivity problem. The sectoral forum model offers some suggestions for the development of policy in the future. If it's good enough for low paid sectors then why shouldn't better performing parts of the economy, where unions have a substantial presence, stand to benefit from social dialogue?

Despite their absence from the Warwick document, a developing conversation about these issues is essential if unions and government are to establish a progressive consensus in the workplace. The terrain is highly political and will inevitably highlight sharp differences between government and opposition. A central task must be to develop a sophisticated articulation of the notion of 'good work'. If successful, the prize for unions is growing membership and a secure future when the Conservatives return to power; the prize for the Government is a transformed labour market, wider opportunities for all and a more cohesive society.

Moving the conversation forward

Government alone cannot take forward this discussion. Someone on the union side needs to exercise leadership. Union modernisers are still slightly stunned by the shift to the left over the last two years and are not quite certain how to respond. People must be given renewed confidence to express views that contradict the new trade union orthodoxy. Organisations like the Fabian Society have a critical role to play, bringing together politicians, left-wing intellectuals and trade unions to discuss the questions raised in this pamphlet.

Those unions grouped under the umbrella of Unions 21 may be able to create some space for a constructive discussion. Community is now playing the leading role in the organisation alongside Connect and Prospect. All three are well-led unions with effective general secretaries and high quality staff with the capacity for radical action. In their different ways, all these organisations exemplify union innovation.

The most important objective is to create an opportunity for people to think, and allow them to learn from each other and reach their own conclusions about how best they can contribute to the process of renewal.

A final word

I did not set out in this pamphlet to write an obituary of the union movement, but to raise some profound questions about the future of organised labour in the UK. I have written elsewhere that freedom of association is a fundamental human right and that at their best trade unions can be academies of citizenship.[33] I stand by these views and hope that my belief in the role that unions play in a democratic society can be detected as the golden thread running through this narrative.

It is fashionable to say that trade unions have no future, that the conditions that gave birth to the movement have disappeared and that a slow withering away is inevitable. I do not share that pessimistic prognosis. Whether trade unions witness resurgence or find themselves on the road to perdition is largely in their own hands. More labour law is not the answer. German unions still benefit from some of the strongest co-determination legislation in the world but membership there is around 20 per cent. French unions operate in a highly regulated labour market and have union density of less than 10 per cent. With the exception of the Nordic countries, union decline can be found under both centre-left and centre-right governments, and in countries with both supportive and hostile public policy.

This means that British unions must confront the harsh realities of membership decline and address tough questions about structure, culture and organisational purpose. It means that unions need to be guided by the evidence of what workers really want, rather than some romantic notion of the incipient radicalism of the working class. In other words, unions must turn their face to the future and, in a questing spirit, adopt the revisionist mindset that Eduard Bernstein recommended for all good social democrats in the late nineteenth century—that there is no substitute for rapid adaptation to social and economic change.[34] Expressed more parochially, it means that unions should respond to the question that Tony Crosland asked of us almost 50 years ago: how can the centre-left find a persuasive narrative in a society where scarcity has largely disappeared, where tastes are differentiated and where old solidarities are eroding? How, in other words, can unions adapt to the modern world?

This does not require us to abandon fundamental principles or betray our history. Contrary to the popular view that society has been thoroughly Thatcherised and that individualism is an inescapable, if unpleasant, fact of life, all the evidence suggests that at least two-thirds of workers have a keen understanding of the logic of collective action. That this is not yet manifested in trade union membership says more about the ability of unions to appeal to today's workforce than it does about individuals' commitment to trade unionism.

Those unions that are growing today point the way for others. Their strategies are adapted to reflect the reality of the 'hour glass' labour market and they have displayed a real capacity for innovation. It would be a tragedy for the unions and Labour if the debate were dominated by a left that believes tomorrow leads merely to a better yesterday.

Britain needs strong, vibrant, responsible and growing unions. We will have a stronger society as a result and stronger foundations on which to build a distinctively British social democracy. The task is urgent. Those of us who believe in union modernisation must advance our case with energy and confidence, marshalling arguments and using evidence to refute the unsupported assertions that shape much of the debate today.

As Keynes pointed out in reference to our economic problems:

[I]f we consistently act on the optimistic hypothesis, this hypothesis will tend to be realised; whilst by acting on the pessimistic hypothesis we can keep ourselves forever in the pit of want.[35]

This is a fine principle to carry with us as we try to revive trade unionism: believing that resurgence is possible can help us to make it so. The alternative is an unattractive prospect, although it will keep historians busy in the future as they investigate 'the strange death of trade union Britain'.

References

1. David Metcalf, 'Trade unions: resurgence or perdition?' in Susan
    Fernie and David Metcalf (eds), *Trade unions: Resurgence or
    Demise* (Routledge, 2005) 115.
2. Barbara Kersley et al, *Inside the Workplace, First Findings from the
    2004 Workplace Employment Relations Survey* (WERS, 2004;
    DTI, 2005).
3. All data is drawn from the Labour Force Survey (Autumn 2004),
    unless otherwise stated.
4. See Mark Cully et al, *Britain at Work* (DTI, 1999).
5. See Jonathan Rose, *The Intellectual Life of the British Working
    Classes* (Yale, 2002)
6. Maarten Goos and Alan Manning, 'McJobs and MacJobs' in Richard
    Dickens et al (ed) *The State of Working Britain* (Palgrave, 2003)
    p 70 et seq.
7. *Ibid.*
8. Gosta Esping-Anderson, 'Inequalities of Incomes and Opportunities'
    in Anthony Giddens and Patrick Diamond (eds), *The New
    Egalitarianism* (Polity, 2005) 8.
9. Neil Millward et al, *All Change at Work* (Routledge, 2000) p.180.
10. Metcalf, *op cit.*
11. One might also note that in countries with strong trade unions the
    wage premium is close to zero because workers will either be
    union members or covered by a collective agreement. It could
    be said that this is a better situation for unions than the exis-
    tence of a large wage premium (as in the USA) where
    employers have more reason to resist union recognition.
12. Alex Bryson, *Union Effects on Managerial and Employee Perceptions
    of Employee Relations in Britain* (Centre for Economic
    Performance, 2001).
13. Cully et al, *op cit.*
14. Eric Hobsbawm, 'The Forward March of Labour Halted?', in Martin

Jacques and Francis Mulhern (eds), *The Forward March of Labour Halted?* (Verso1981) p.2. A cynic would say that Hobsbawm dates the 'halt' to the period when the Communist tide began to recede in British trade unions.

15. *Ibid*, p.8. This is no longer an accurate characterisation of the UK's 'flexible' labour market, where wages are effectively determined by market conditions. In the absence of effective unions employers have significant discretion over how much they pay— similar workers doing similar jobs can have very different pay packages.

16. C.A.R. Crosland, *The Future of Socialism* (Jonathan Cape, 1956).

17. Robert Taylor, *Britain's World of Work: Myths and Realities* (ESRC, 2002).

18. *Employment Outlook* (OECD ,2001).

19. Kersley et al *WERS 2004*, op cit.

20. Michael Marmot, *Status Syndrome* (Bloomsbury, 2004).

21. See, Paul Willman, 'Circling the Wagons: Endogeneity in Union Decline', in Fernie and Metcalf (eds), op cit, p.45.

22. Ibid, p.56.

23. In this case 'smaller' means those with fewer than 350,000-400,000 members.

24. It could be said that Unison have already embraced this principle through their close working relationship with the FDA, the union for senior civil servants.

25. Paul Thompson et al, 'The Future of Unions and Labour Relations', *Renewal*, 13:1 (2005).

26. Warwick Policy Forum, Section 3: 'Full employment and working in modern Britain' (The Labour Party, 2004),

27. *Ibid*.

28. See *Partners for Progress: Next Steps for the New Unionism* (TUC, 1997).

29. David Coats, 'Murder, Divorce or a Trial Separation?', in *Renewal*, 13:1 (2005).

30. Rt Hon Tony Blair MP, 'Renewing the party in government', speech to Progress conference, 15 October 2005.
31. See David Coats, *An Agenda for Work* (The Work Foundation, 2005).
32. R.H. Tawney, *Equality* (George Allen and Unwin, 1929).
33. See David Coats, *Speaking Up!* (The Work Foundation, 2004).
34. Bernstein, *Evolutionary Socialism* (1899, Shocken edition, 1961).
35. J.M. Keynes, *Preface to Essays in Persuasion* (1931, Norton edition, 1963) p.vii.

Acknowledgments

I would like to thank Sunder Katwala, Richard Brooks and Jonathan Heawood at the Fabian Society for their insightful comments and invaluable editorial support. John Monks offered some typically trenchant views on an early draft. As ever, I bear full responsibility for the text.